ECLECTIC
Poetic

R. A. Gilmore

ISBN: 979-8-9872766-1-7

Table of Contents

Preface

God has been, and is, my inspiration for the writing of poems. Letting God lead in this process has been very rewarding and the results are pleasing to the eye, and to the ear. While I perform the writing, I'm more and more convinced that the true author of the poems is God.

I'm thankful for the privilege and opportunity to participate in this joint venture with the Lord. While I bear the responsibility for the written words, all honor and glory, if any, goes to God.

For this collection of fifty-one poems, I trust you find them enjoyable and perhaps some will even challenge your thinking.

God is the poet,
I am the recording secretary.

R. A. Gilmore

Foreword

I first met Dick Gilmore several years ago, when he joined me on a group trip to India where we spent time at the Sat Tal Christian Ashram, founded by the missionary-evangelist E. Stanley Jones. Participating in a Christian Ashram is a tremendous experience that inspires the transformation of persons to be followers of Jesus Christ, and discover, renew, and deepen their relationship with God, themselves, and others.

Dick was immediately at home in this setting and set about listening to God and writing poetry. I could see him each day on the verandah filling pages with precious words about his experience, which he generously shared with others. He has now written more than 3,000 poems and published four books of his own poems. This book is the fifth!

When Dick asked me to write a foreword to his new book of poetry, I was looking forward to reading what God had in mind, for Dick generously acknowledges that *God is the poet, he is merely the recording secretary.*

This book's intriguing title, *Eclectic Poetic* captures both whimsy and freedom as Dick's inspired words illustrate that poetry knows no bounds when it comes to subject matter and even more so when the Spirit both inspires and guides the words.

Dick is intensely grateful for the variety life offers us, and hopes that these poetic verses will offer entertainment, occasions of thoughtfulness, and appeal to the reader's curiosity about the unusual and serendipitous vagaries of life. Embracing the eclectic, including both the random and the complex can offer us a fresh and novel opportunity to rediscover Christ's presence in their midst, and gain fresh understanding of God's transforming grace in all our experiences in life.

Join me in embracing two of these serendipitous (and enchanting) gifts of eclectic poetic grace: *The Brother-Sister Saga* and *Time*.

Anne Mathews-Younes, Ed.D., D.Min.
President, E. Stanley Jones Foundation
www.estanleyjonesfoundation.com

Introduction

According to Webster's III International Dictionary, the word "eclectic" means composed of elements drawn from various sources. That is the case for this collection of poems. Poetry knows no bounds when it comes to subject matter. That statement is borne out by the poems included in this volume.

The seven sections are assorted in content, ranging from riddles, science, varied, through music. The numbers of poems in each section ranges from three (Unusual and Music) to fifteen (Varied). The poems in each section are singular poems that stand alone. The one exception is the section titled Mary's Journey. These are related and are sequential in their presentation.

The scriptural notation for each section is a construct to demonstrate that the section titles are words that are found in the Bible. The scripture cited has nothing to do with

the contents of the section. The references
serve to tie the material together.
Trust these poems will provide you
entertainment, thoughtfulness, and appeal to
your spirit.

Riddles

For understanding proverbs and parables, the sayings and riddles of the wise.

Proverbs 1:6
(New International Version)

Life is full of problems, puzzles and/or riddles. The riddles can challenge our thinking and they can provide entertainment. They can also serve to hone our thinking skills. Riddles can also help us see through those words that are used to confuse us or obfuscate us.

Riddles are to challenge your thought processes. The first seven riddles are straight forward. The eighth is a riddle within one of the first seven riddles. The challenge is to find the riddle and then solve it.

Riddle 1

One bright spot when I'm aglow
May be all I have to show.
I'm short, I'm fat, I'm tall, I'm thin
Most any shape you'll find me in.
There's no relation 'tween height and girth;
I'm used in sorrow, in love, in mirth.
My sides are often straight when I am new,
They can get rough in a minute or two.
There are times while in use I can bend quite
    nice,
But use me while leaning is not good advice.
I can stand alone or in a cluster
Or any arrangement you can muster.
I have been able to shed some light
When things are grim or you're in a plight.
I do my thing, what e'er my use,
Be careful though and don't abuse.
To some I'm really adored,
Others think that I'm abhorred.

Riddle 2

Alone I'm very seldom found.
You never find me on the ground.
I'm measured out most frequently.
My signature's not truly me.
I never beat, always beaten.
You'll find me used so very often.
I'm used in grief, joy, in sorrow.
I'll be used somewhere tomorrow.
My size, shape are often varied.
When some use me they get harried.
Sometimes you'll find that I am tied
To a friend that is at my side.
An accidental guess, you see,
Would not reveal just who I be.

Riddle 3

I greet each day with brilliant smile,
That is seen for many a mile.
Sometimes I will just hide my face,
It's not a game, not a disgrace.
A comfort and a warmth I give
To all those kinds of things that live.
I rise each day and sleep at night.
I have no eyes and hence no sight.

Riddle 4

Floating high on tether's tip,
Bobbing as the breezes dip,
Striving hard to reach the sky,
Bouncing as the day goes by.

As the hours do race along,
I soon droop amid the throng.
The taut line begins to slack,
To the earth I do drift back.

Now my billowed sides are flat,
On the ground is where I'm at.
Exhausted now is my breath.
This has brought about my death.

Riddle 5

If I have hands, they're on display.
I'm correct at least twice a day.
Sometimes I never make a sound.
Dependence on me is profound.

Sometimes my face does brightly glow.
Sometimes I have no face to show.
Sometimes I'm blank and numberless.
Sometimes I have buttons to press.

I can make noise if me you set.
Sometimes I quit if I get wet.
Quite often you do look at me,
Rarely do you like what you see.

I can do things that may astound.
In many places I am found.
To me please do not show pity
Do you know my identity?

Riddle 6

Around and around it does go;
Sometimes it's fast, sometimes it's slow.
It responds to its master's hand,
Heeding each and ev'ry command.

It has one path to circumscribe,
It stays the course, won't take a bribe.
With outstretched arms it does await
For the call to display its trait.

In silence it does wait or go,
And never tries to be the show.
Its faithfulness we do assume,
And when it fails, we really fume.

(Written while visiting Carleen and John Alderman
in Lewisville, TX)

Riddle 7

I have a head, but have no feet.
I have a bed, but never sleep.
I've no money, but visit banks.
I've no appointments I should keep.

I am what you would call quite cool.
You need me for you to have life.
Sometimes I can be very hot.
Too much of me can bring you strife.

I can run and sometimes I fall.
Sometimes I'm fast, sometimes I'm slow.
I'm mostly calm, but can be wild.
I know where I'm supposed to go.

Can you decipher this riddle?
Can you discern what I might be?
Don't be too hard upon yourself
As you wrestle with this ditty.

Riddle 8

Of the seven riddles you've tried
One has a riddle that's inside.
If you saw it, please do not tell,
Let others on it thus to dwell.

It is something beyond the norm,
Yet it is an accepted form.
It's something that will ever count
As curiosity does mount.

For many they will never know
Just what this one riddle does show.
Puzzle-solving skill it will test.
Be sure your mind's had lots of rest.

Science

O Timothy, keep that which is committed to thy trust, turn away from profane voices and vain things and arguments in the vain name of science.
1 Timothy 6:20
(Jubilee Bible 2000)

SCIENCE poems are a wide variety of parts of the broad field of science. While this section may not stir your heart or brain, read through them to get some sense of the complexities of science.

The poem on statistics: I was asked to teach statistics to nursing students. Knowing their abject fear of the subject, and their abhorrence of the word statistics, the poem was written from the students' perspective. The poem was read to the class as the first item on the first day. The intent was to put

them at ease and to help them understand
that most of the numbers they would use
daily as normal values were actually
statistical averages.

Statistics

Statistics is a ten-letter word,
One of the worst I've ever heard.
Its use I have steadfast refused
Because its ways leave me confused.

Terms like mean, median, mode
Nothing but ill for me do bode.
Variable dependent or independent
Are things for which I have no penchant.

Chi-squared test and t-test too —
What am I supposed to do?
Distribution normal, but slightly skewed
Makes me think that I've been stewed!

Standard deviation of the mean
And variance are often seen.
Hypothesis testing we're asked to do.
I'm fouled by errors type one and two!

Relationships of cause - effect
Make me think I should defect.
Contributory, contingent, alternative
Are terms with which I cannot live.

Now I've made my tirade known
For statistics I am not prone.
I'm bent and broken for all to see —
I find statistics I use daily.

Enzymes

In pedagogically presenting the enzyme
    kinetic,
I endeavor to be lucid and not at all frenetic.
Velocities, rate constants and reactant
    concentration,
Provide for the derivation of the Michaelis-
    Menten equation.

A double reciprocal provides not a shirk,
Resulting in a form called Lineweaver-
    Burke.
Operate with V max and you'll have to
    agree,
The resultant is none other than Eadie-
    Hofstee.

We use these forms for frequent instruction,
But need to point out it's just introduction.
From the realities of life you'll not be
    abated,
Most enzyme reactions are quite
    complicated.

Reactions with multisubstrates are normal,
Derivations of these are really quite formal.
The many types of these mechanisms,
Should not be the source or start of schisms.

Ordered, random, and also ping-pong,
With Uni, Bi, and Ter go along.
Having all this now under the belt,
Changes in enzymic activity will be dealt.

Factors are pH and the effect of heat,
But inhibitors are things that are really neat.
With these you can help in turning the tide,
About what an enzyme is doing inside.

Inhibition can occur in many a way –
Competitive, noncompetitive, uncompetitive
    they play.
All are reversible and mathematically
    amenable,
For deriving equations – but for this class
    unthinkable.

Enzyme discussion would be incomplete
If irreversible inhibition we did delete.
Quantitative assay of enzymic activity,
We discuss in a tone of pedantic civility.

Activity units and purified preps,
Are best determined in sequential steps.
Enzymes, substrates and cofactor
    complexes,
Need not at all ever perplex us.

Specificity, functionality, efficiency
    catalytic,
Active site mechanisms of reactions
    enzymatic.
Regulatory, allosteric, covalent modulation,
And isozymes are part of intracellular
    regulation.

Cofactors play a role that's important you'll
    see,
Some enzymes won't function without their
    vitamin B.
Thiamin, flavin, and acid lipoic,
Are presented in terms that are not quite
    stoic.

Nicotinic, folic, biotin and CoA,
Are used by the enzymes to have things their
way.
That's what's involved in things of the
enzyme,
And that is the end of this biochemical
rhyme.

Metric Lament

They talk about liters and I'm using quarts.
They say kilometers when I see just miles.
Temperature is now Celsius degrees,
But for me Fahrenheit can bring in the
    smiles.

The friendly old inch is no longer in style;
The centimeter has now come into vogue.
The yard and yardstick have now been
    replaced.
If you use rod you are considered a rogue.

The link and the chain and the furlong are
    gone;
The pole and the perch have been laid to
    their rest.
The acre, section and township are no more.
The are and the hectare are now what is best.

The gill, the ounce and the pint and the
    gallon,
The barrel, the bushel and even the peck,
Are like the old soldiers, they never will die,
But they'll be like a millstone around my
    neck.

The nautical measure is stated in leagues,
In feet or in fathoms or cable's length too.
Like all the others when conversion's
    complete,
These cherished old friends will disappear
    from view.

The femto, pico, the milli and the deci,
The tera, giga, the mega and kilo
Are prefixes I'll come to handle with ease,
But I'd rather stay with the ones that I know.

A Symposium

Down in the hills of eastern Tennessee,
To that city which deals in energy,
People did descend from many diff'rent
    land.
To bring to dosimetry a helping hand.

Radiopharmaceuticals were in mind
And those of course were of many different
    kind.
Not all would agree on every single point,
But all did agree that efforts should be joint.

Nuclide distribution, dose calculation,
Human data handling, dose estimation,
Extrapolation, kinetics, models too,
Were the session topics which we did
    imbue.

Questions did arise, but in a friendly tone.
These were helpful for our own ideas to
hone.
A panel summarized what transpired that
week,
Then all did depart for more answers to
seek.

(Written while attending the Third International
Radiopharmaceutical Dosimetry Symposium,
in Oak Ridge, TN)

28

Solar Bodies

The sphere proceeds on its orbit.
Soon it reaches its apogee.
It passes through and then descends
Racing towards its perigee.

The oblate spheroid keeps on track
Heading for its aphelion.
It passes through and then descends
Speeding to its perhelion.

The oblate spheroid does revolve
With no sign of hesitation.
Yet the axis on which it spins
Endures a defined precession.

The ecliptic's a busy place
With much elliptical action.
Many bodies interact in
Graceful mutual attraction.

(Notes: the sphere is the moon;
the oblate spheroid is the earth;
the ecliptic is the plane of the solar system)

Technology

In technology we do trust,
Sometimes its ways boggle our mind.
We think nothing about its ways
Until there's something we can't find.

We're flustered, upset, wonder why
This machine won't do what we ask.
We try this and then call for help
Because it won't do today's task.

We yield unto a last resort
And reconstruct the high-tech route.
We get things restored, do some work
And wonder what just came about.

(Written at the Donelson-Hermitage YMCA)

Unusual

The islanders showed us unusual kindness. They built a fire and welcomed us all because it was raining and cold. Paul gathered a pile of brushwood and, as he put it on the fire, a viper, driven out by the heat, fastened itself on his hand. When the islanders saw the snake hanging from his hand, they said to each other, "This man must be a murderer; for though he escaped from the sea, the goddess Justice has not allowed him to live." But Paul shook the snake off into the fire and suffered no ill effects. The people expected him to swell up or suddenly fall dead; but after waiting a long time and seeing nothing unusual happen to him, they changed their minds and said he was a god.

Acts 28:2-6
(New International Version)

31

Our life is confronted by unusual happenings which may seem to baffle us. In many instances these unusual happenings are really usual things in a different context. We should set our life's base on our firm foundation and not be overly concerned about unusual happenings.

The three poems in the section titled UNUSUAL may test your mettle. The second of these three poems may leave you wondering. If so, look at Appendix 3 for some help.

Dessert Ditty

Dulcet desserts, delectable, desirous,
Daintily decorate dinners delicious.
Dichotomy dwells during decision –
Dare defect diet dedication?
Duly defy debilitation?
Decry desserts, decrease dyspepsia!
Debar desserts, delay dysplasia!

The Brother-Sister Saga

This is the saga of Dip and Sara;
Brother and sister, they hang together.
She is the eldest, but not very much,
And neither one is much of a bother.

Sometimes they stumble or reach a dead end
As they meander to seek and to find.
There are great times when a neat thing
   happens
Because each of them is quite sharp of mind.

They often head out but have to detour
Due to an obstacle along the way.
They don't get discouraged or faint of heart,
Yet unique things happen most ev'ry day.

Wonderful things seem often to happen,
In the country and even the city.
These two accompany people like you.
Their full names are Sara and Dip Ity.

Jesus Is A Mathematician

Jesus uses mathematics
And He uses statistics too.
Examples are found in the Word
And we know the Word is true.

Addition's a good place to start
Because it is easy to do.
It is found in Matthew and Luke:
These things will be added to you.[1]

Subtraction has a helpful role
That now and then comes into play.
In seed planting, some fell by the
Side where birds carried them away.[2]

Multiplication's also there,
Not by chance but by decision.
The faith was to be multiplied
Through what's called the Great
    Commission.[3]

We don't like the division part,
But it's a piece that does matter.
Christ came to divide family
With a man against his father.[4]

Chaos theory is found in Mark
And Christ used it in His teaching.
Weeping, wailing in the darkness,
And teeth set on edge with gnashing.[5]

Christ instructed with equation
So to help the people know.
The only thing that you can reap
Is based upon the seed you sow.[6]

Calculus too is used by Christ,
Matthew has the integral part.
The offer is open to all
Who invite Christ into their heart.[7]

The differential calculus
Is one that Christ carefully notes.
He differentiates two groups
As He separates sheep from goats.[8]

Fractions will now be considered,
For they are a part of Christ's lore.
Remember what Zacchaeus did?
He gave half of his all to the poor.[9]

Return on investment is found
In the books of Luke and Matthew.
It does provide serious thought
That gives your mind something to chew.[10]

Some outcomes are predictable.
Unless your righteousness is more
Than of the Scribes and Pharisees,
You'll not see what God has in store.[11]

Math requires there be solutions,
And Christ does have one for our strife.
He can settle our troubled hearts:
I'm the way, the truth and the life.[12]

Christ uses math in His teachings
And these apply to everyone.
It helps us in our Christian walk
To be sure that God's will is done.

1. Matthew 6:33; Luke 12:31
2. Matthew 13:4
3. Matthew 28:19-20
4. Matthew 10:35-36
5. Mark 13:8-25

6. Matthew 13:24-30
7. Matthew 11:28
8. Matthew 25:32
9. Luke 19:8
10. Matthew 13:23; Luke 19:19-26
11. Matthew 5:20
12. John 14:6

Mary's Journey

Now Joseph also went up from Galilee, from the city of Nazareth, to Judea, to the city of David which is called Bethlehem, because he was of the house and family of David, in order to register along with Mary, who was betrothed to him, and was pregnant.

Luke 2:4-5
(New American Standard Bible)

Mary and Joseph made the journey and there is support for that. Each of us undertake journeys, even if that journey is only to the grocery. Sometimes our journey is based on our need, sometimes the journey is job-related, perhaps a transfer to another city. Sometimes the journey may be to another location for educational pursuits.

39

The series of eight poems titled *Mary's Journey* portrays Mary's experience as she and Joseph travelled to Bethlehem to register for the census. There is very little scriptural reference for these poems. They are a combination of the author's imagination, practical aspects of such a journey, and the concerns of a young mother-to-be as she undertakes the journey.

On The Move

The whole country was in astir
Because of the Roman decree.
People were planning for the trip
And they could stay with family.

While all this hub-bub did ensue
Sages were agitated too.
With all of this activity
Could God be planning something new?

For ages on tales had been told
But no one knew the time or where.
Now the Spirit was on the move,
O Lord God help us to prepare.

(Written while at Covenant Presbyterian Church,
Nashville, TN)

Mary's Lament

A five-day trek across the land?
I'm weary now, can hardly stand.
What if this baby wants to be born
While we're on this trip so forlorn?

Oh if Elizabeth were here
To help me through this time so drear.
She'd know just what I ought to do
So the babe and I could get through.

It's Joseph, the babe, God and me –
The four of us are family.
O Lord protect us as we roam
Take us safely to David's home.

(Written while at Covenant Presbyterian Church,
Nashville, TN)

42

Getting Started

The dark of night was holding fast
As if to dare dawn to appear.
Kind gentle words from Joseph's voice
Fell softly upon Mary's ear.

It was time to begin the trip
To David's home, the House of Bread.
Young Mary who was great with child
Wanted to rest her weary head.

The caravan did set the pace
And Mary's donkey followed true.
She pondered the angel's sweet words
Of what God was going to do.

(Written while at Covenant Presbyterian Church,
Nashville, TN)

Settling In

It seems we're getting settled in
Away from the Nazareth din.
The weather's been much like at home,
Making it easier to roam.

We joined another caravan
Which was something Joseph did plan.
Mild discomfort along the way
Was masked by donkey's gentle sway.

The babe adjusted rather quick
And very rarely gave a kick.
That was a comfort to my heart,
For the trip it was a good start.

Hannah's Help

Camping along the way at night
You see so many stars so bright.
They're like God's angels watching o'er
And His great love they outward pour.

The babe's been quiet for these days
Which brings a comfort to my ways.
Serenity of home and bed
Seems to keep dancing in my head.

Met Hannah as we travelled on
And knew that soon she would be gone.
She will stay at Jerusalem
As we move on to Bethlehem.

Hannah brought much relief to life
When I found she was a midwife.
Such a great comfort she did bring,
It made my weary heart to sing.

Time Is Nigh

For days we were in hills so grand,
Now it's the valley full of sand.
The day's not subject to heat's rule,
The night is brisk and not too cool.

The donkey doesn't seem to mind
As along the trail we do wind.
To check on me, Hannah drops by.
She told me that my time is nigh.

Lord God to You I humbly pray
That in my womb the babe will stay
'Till we get to Bethlehem town
And settled where we will bed down.

In Bethlehem

Bethlehem's gates relieved our mind.
A place to stay we now must find.
No Hannah here to help me through
As it seems the baby is due.

Joseph set out to find a room
For us and the babe in my womb.
He spent much time, looked ev'rywhere.
The search soon put us in despair.

A stable was the only site
That we could find to spend the night.
It was warm, away from the din,
And there was no room at the inn.

Mary's Plea

How amazing these past few months
With ev'rything that did transpire.
Now here I am with babe in arms
What each maiden's heart does desire.

The visitation of the angel,
Elizabeth being with child,
Joseph yielding unto God's will,
Keeping me from being defiled.

There was that trip to Bethlehem
And finding no room at the inn.
A stable stall and manger bed
Was where her babe's life did begin.

The announcement from the heav'ns
As the angelic choir did sing.
Visits by the near-by shepherds
And the obeisance they did bring.

What lies ahead for this wee babe
And for Joseph and for me too?
O Lord please guide us in our ways
For we do not know what to do.

Varied

Do not be misled by varied and strange teachings; for it is good for the heart to be strengthened by grace, not by foods, through which those who were so occupied were not benefited.
Hebrews 13:9
(New American Standard Bible)

We can be thankful for variety in life which helps us grow and perhaps expands our horizons. We sometimes encounter varied perspectives in our faith journey. Working through these perspectives helps us grow in our faith. The same can be said for our professional undertakings.

Rain, Rein, Reign

The heavy drops once more are lain
Providing drink to thirsty plain.
If puddles form it is a pain,
Yet it all happens with the rain.

Wild horses gallop the terrain
And they are difficult to train.
Treat them gently with love and grain
And they will submit to the rein.

Christ's death on the cross, it was gain
For He removed our guilty stain.
Sinful ones He does not disdain.
O'er all our life He does reign.

Birthday Greetings

It's a wondrous glorious day,
A time to shout hip hip hooray.
It is the one day of the year
For special joy and special cheer.

It is the time for you to boast
That on this day you are the most.
It's the day to receive your due;
It's the day that's all about you.

Relax, enjoy and have great fun.
On this day you are number one.
It's the day to be full of glee
And you can say, "It's all about me!"

God did rejoice when you were born.
Angels in heaven blew their horn.
God designed this day just for you.
God still celebrates this day too.

Now it's your time to celebrate.
Because you're special and so great,
Everything should go your way,
So you'll have a HAPPY BIRTHDAY.

Time

Time, the invader of our life.
It mediates and brings us strife.
It soothes and it befuddles too
And impacts ev'rything we do.

Often it seems it does us stalk,
And it is frequent in our talk.
We take some time because we care,
And it is time that we do share.

We make the time to do our stuff,
We waste our time on just some fluff.
We do use time to do our will,
And we pass time by sitting still.

We have time to do what we would.
We buy time whenever we could.
We devote time for being kind.
We wait for time when in a bind.

Through it all time does never change,
And time maintains a constant range.
Each has the same amount of time.
Time is precious, treat it as prime.

(Written while flying from Minneapolis/St. Paul,
MN to San Diego, CA)

Covered Bridge

The old covered bridge spanned the stream
Making dry the trip o'er the way.
The gabled roof provided shade
From summer sun's harsh beating ray.

The clip-clop of the horse's hooves
Echoed around those rustic beams.
Oh, how that sound did make a change
When on the old road's dusty seams.

Winter brought a special effect
When snow bedecked the countryside.
No clippity-clop could be heard
'Till into the bridge you would ride.

Memories are all that remain
Of wagon, buggy and the sleigh
That horses pulled along the path
And through the covered bridge archway.

The Gathering Place

They gather in the massive hall.
Though some be short and some be tall
They each persue their mission call
To visit a specific stall.

Many gather in this mahal
And each does have their own cabal.
Some seem to be having a ball,
They move so quick and never fall.

They tote their bags, some great, some
    small,
They do it with joy, not a pall,
As they gaze at every wall.
They are the shoppers at the mall.

(Written while sitting in Green Hills Mall,
Nashville, TN)

Rush Hour Traffic

Cars, trucks, and vans, and SUVs,
Semis and some school buses too,
Hieing along in tandem file,
Striving all the lights to get through.

Order is the rule of the road
As these progress along the way.
The goal is to arrive safely
At the start of another day.

Slowly they move, or just sit still;
Daily they each do play this game.
While on to work they do progress,
Rush hour traffic seems a wrong name.

(Written while waiting for the barber shop to open)

The Spots

Golden rays pass through the windows
Casting bright spots around the room.
The spots migrate along the way
As if they're pushed by a slow broom.

They are silent interlopers,
Tiptoeing on the edge of stairs.
A sweet warm caress they do plant
On walls, floors and even the chairs.

Their final act is to climb walls,
Kissing each stone along the way.
Those bright spots begin to grow dim,
Then they're gone 'till another day.

(Written while sitting in the sanctuary of
Covenant Presbyterian Church, Nashville, TN,
during the early evening)

Faithful Friends

Each morning they always greet me,
Always sitting in those two chairs.
Never failing in their presence,
With their sweet smiles and loving stares.

Their quiet demeanor's unique,
Their solitude does solace share.
Their countenance does never change,
No matter what, they always care.

Just like Job's friends in that first week,
These two sit silent all the day.
Unlike Job's friends who then did speak,
These never have a word to say.

(Raggedy Ann and Raggedy Andy are each in their
small rockers in our sitting room)

Chuck Wagon

Nestled at the foot of the bluff
The chuck wagon has found a place
To set its camp and build its fire
To which the cowpokes soon will race.

The wood's in place, the spit is set.
The kettles hang in their array.
The fire crackles, glows so bright.
The chuck master does hold full sway.

A sweet aroma fills the air
And wafts gently across the plain.
Cowpokes ride in and find a log
To rest and their strength to regain.

(Reflections on the Harvey Johnson
painting "Chowtime in Montana"
at the Cheekwood Gallery, Nashville, TN)

The Fireplace

The andirons so stately stand
Embracing their cache of big logs.
The blackened firebricks that surround
Are ready for a blaze so grand.

The hearth and mantle, all of stone,
Present such an elegant scene.
Though scarred by time and fires of yore,
Its setting will not be outgrown.

Memories of times long ago
Are harbored in this unique place.
Great stories and tales do abound
When the fireplace is all aglow.

(Written while sitting in front of the top floor
fireplace at the Cheekwood Gallery)

The Fountain

The fountain's stream does spurt on high.
Into the basin it does drop.
The droplets dance across the pool
In a stream that never does stop.

The basin slowly drips its stuff
In a gentle soothing cascade.
The water flows from the small pool
Dribbling down in its own parade.

The lower pool receives the flow
In a scene of such tender grace.
It all provides such solitude
And a time of much slower pace.

(Written while sitting near the fountain
at the Cheekwood Gallery)

The Stream

The little steam does gently flow
Spilling over the rocky path.
Some places it gurgles along
Never flowing with any wrath.

It slips across a large flat rock
Then silently flows o'er the rim.
It has its course between the stones
Which is so very neat and trim.

Always following its set course,
Into the pond it makes its way.
Persistent, but never rushing,
It's like a little child at play.

(Written while sitting beside the little stream at
Cheekwood Botanical Garden)

Mighty Have Fallen

A reign of terror was unleashed
Upon the mighty rankings beast.
Those that were high did lose their seat
As they were humbled in defeat.

For some it was a day of thanks,
Upsetting those of higher ranks.
For those sitting high and lofty
Were roasted like a bland turkey.

For some it was another day
To take the field, enjoy the play.
They rose up high as in days past
Establishing themselves so fast.

The fickleness of ranking trust
Resulted in atrocious bust.
Many now are very sullen
As mighty ones now have fallen.

(There were some major upsets in the college
football games this day – November 23, 2013)

Acedia

Unannounced this demon creeps in,
Oft considered a mortal sin.
Many a victim it does claim,
Acedia its proper name.

When acedia comes your way
You cannot work and cannot pray.
You're saddled with a lack of care,
Yet with no one you want to share.

The word is old, now rarely seen,
And no one wants its ugly sheen.
It is a flight from the divine,
You'll lack desire to even whine.

Holy, Wholly, Holey

God informed us He is holy,[1]
He calls us to be holy too.[2]
We're to be holy at all times
And be holy in all we do.[3]

God, make us wholly full of light[4]
So on others Your light will shine.
Let the light be wholly of You
And that we would be wholly Thine.[5]

Lord, make us be holey people
So that we are much like a sieve.
Then as You fill us with Your love
Love will drip ev'rywhere we live.

---

1. Leviticus 11:45
2. 1 Peter 1:16
3. 1 Peter 1:15
4. Luke 11:34
5. 1 Kings 8:61

Music

Speaking to one another with psalms, hymns, and songs from the Spirit. Sing and make music from your heart to the Lord.
Ephesians 5:19
(New International Version).

Music enters many spheres of our life. For some it is professional, for some it is a diversion. For others it can be an opportunity to serve and give back. There are those who enjoy listening and watching musical performances to enhance their own appreciation for life.

Music

Music soothes the savage beast, as the
    saying goes.
Defining just what music is may bring some
    to blows.
What music is for some is noise to many
    other.
What for one does soothe, for a second is a
    bother.

Rock takes on several forms – acid, hard or
    plain;
Bluegrass, country or western though may
    bring you much less pain.
Folk music and popular are heard from day
    to day,
With some old favorites coming back in
    slightly new array.

Operettas and musicals occasionally will be
   heard,
But modern music and electronic sound are
   the latest word.
Semi-classics for many is what they like to
   hear,
And classical music is what others hold
   dear.

Chamber music to some is a type that stands
   apart.
Opera and cantata are what others take to
   heart.
Gospel songs may be all types, hymns may
   be quite staid,
And canticles and chants make some folk
   seem afraid.

Music takes on many forms from notes upon
   a page –
Soothing one, inspiring one and sending one
   to rage.
Just like the famous saying about beauty that
   we hear,
Music to the hearer is what he lets in his ear.

Heritage

It's a state that's narrow and long
With a great history of song.
Mountains and rivers are the source
That set the music on its course.

The year eighteen seventy one
Was the start of the music run.
Fisk Jubilee Singers were first
As music on the scene did burst.

Nashville then was the music place,
Wearing the crown with style and grace.
For forty years that star shone bright,
Then other places showed their light.

Memphis was next to join the show,
Chattanooga also did glow,
With jazz, blues, and rock-n-roll,
White gospel sound and even soul.

The Barn Dance and Grand Ole Opry
With foot stompin tunes from country
In the twenties joined in the game,
Adding to Nashville's fame.

In late twenties another place
Became known as a music base.
Bristol's star did shine ever bright
As it was the recording site.

Mountains in the east did abound
With string bands and the fiddle sound.
Those mountains gave another choice
As Celtic heritage did voice.

Thirties to fifties did embrace
Knoxville as the recording place
And country music broadcasting center.
Memphis did recordings later.

The forties had Nashville quite strong
Writing and publishing in song.
In the fifties Nashville became
The recording crossroads of fame.

Many a music well known name
From this state has risen to fame.
They were the ones who set the trend
And each one's star did ascend.

Heritage is a blessed thing
And many voices rose to sing.
Music is still a special part
Imbedded in Tennessee's heart.

By the Numbers

It's the numbers that really count.
Sometimes those numbers sure do mount.
At times those numbers set you free,
Yet they can be more than you see.

Two hundred twenty eight are there.
Sixteen of them stand as a pair.
Sixty two as trios stand,
But only ten as singles grand.

One set of three is quite apart.
Thirty six is another start
That's made of groups of three and two
And these are quite easy to view.

There is a group of fifty two
And these do stand in a bright hue.
Three hundred nineteen is the sum
And together they are not mum.

Take a slightly different view
To picture the whole from the few.
Don't let numbers lead you astray
In this unique numbers array.

Three are pedals made for your feet.
The eighty eight keys are so neat.
Two hundred twenty eight are strings;
That is why the piano sings.

(Written while visiting Marilyn and Tom Dumm at
Lake Chautauqua, NY)

Special

But you are a chosen people, a royal priesthood, a holy nation, God's special possession, that you may declare the praises of him who called you out of darkness into his wonderful light.

1 Peter 2:9
(New International Version)

Each of us have special happenings that give us enjoyment for our life. We cherish such happenings and they can provide wonderful memories that we can revisit and enjoy time and time again.

The section titled SPECIAL is a variety of poems that touch on the vagaries of life.

The Majestic Tree

O stately tree whose branches spread
So thick and far and wide,
For scores of years you stood right there
Storing mem'ries inside.
You knew this land in wilderness,
When all around was wild.
You've seen it go through many change
And now it's tame and mild.
Could you but tell of days of old,
The hist'ry and the lore,
What fascinating things we'd learn
From your great treasure store.

I'll speculate on days gone by
And things you might have heard;
The joy, the peace, the happiness,
And pain that you've endured.
Many a creature, great and small,
Traversed beneath your bough.
The wind and rain and snow and ice
Have danced upon your brow.
The gentle breeze and sunshine bright
Each tender leaf have kissed.
Jack Frost, with his quite varied hues,
Each year has never missed.

Did bears make tracks around your roots
And gently nudge you, too?
Did buffalo graze beneath your arms
And seek some shade from you?
Your branches must have held the birds –
Cradled many a nest.
Other creatures romped in your limbs
Or came to you for rest.
And what about the graceful deer –
Did they around you slink,
To make sure harm was not around,
Before they went to drink?

Did you see the Indian brave
Stealthily hunt his prey?
Maybe a tribe would camp near you
When they came by this way.
Have lovers strolled by hand in hand
Just gazing at the view?
Perchance they stole their first kiss then,
While standing next to you.
Have children climbed your leafy boughs
And hugged you with their arms?
Perhaps you held a swing for them
And thrilled them with your charms.

You gently waved your arms at me,
An invitation made.
Majestic tree what peace you give
Just sitting in your shade.
The rustling of your many leaves
Is wisp'ring in my ear
That you enjoy the time like this,
Just having me so near.
Will I, just enjoying this view
In your great company,
Be a part of your treasure trove
In your posterity?

(Written while visiting Tom and Marilyn Dumm
at Lake Chautauqua, NY)

God Stepped In

History was moving along at its pace,
Caught up in it was the whole human race.
Mankind was sure he'd ultimately win,
But then in moment God did step in.

From years long gone by mankind had been
   told.
The message was scorned for man was so
   bold.
Man carried on in his plight and his sin,
And as was written, 'twas then God stepped
   in.

In a little town it happened one night,
And a single star shone ever so bright.
In a lowly stable, in a small bin,
Was where in majesty God did step in.

Sages of old saw that shining bright star
And followed it on journey afar
To that little stable behind the inn
Where God in His glory had just stepped in.

The shepherds watching their flocks in the
 night,
Awed by that glorious heavenly sight,
Heard the magnanimous angelic din
Announcing the fact that God had stepped
 in.

Into man's history God did step in,
He sent His son as a savior from sin.
As we celebrate His birth on this day
Ask Christ into your life to show the way.

Listen

Listen to the birds when they're singing
  their sweet song.
Listen to the wind as it gently blows along.
Listen to the stream as it bubbles down the
  hill.
Listen intently my friend, be quiet, be still.

Hear the squirrels chatter as they romp in the
  trees.
Hear the chipmunks squeal playing in fallen
  leaves.
Hear the bees a-buzzing 'round flowers
  everywhere.
Hear the sounds of nature as they float in the
  air.

Harken to the cricket who plays a constant
  tune.
Harken to the bull frog as to his mate he'll
  croon.
Harken to the rain as it taps upon the
  ground.
Harken to nature's sounds you can hear all
  around.

Listen to the waterfall in its thund'rous roar.
Listen to the waves as they break upon the
shore.
Listen to the storm with its wind and thunder
clap.
Listen to the quiet and let it you entrap.

Listen to the quiet as it falls on your ear.
Listen to the sound of a gently falling tear.
Listen, harken, hear, it's something we need
to do.
Listen for the voice of God as He speaks to
you.

Opposites

God proclaimed His loving decree.
Satan just smiled, said wait and see.
God's plan, from sin to set men free.
Satan said man belongs to me.

God sent His Son to man on earth.
Satan smiled with sardonic mirth.
Christ a babe in manger bed,
Satan cajoled, He'll be misled.

That babe to Egypt God then sent
To avoid Satan's wild intent.
As a youth Christ was in God's house.
Satan worked, Christ's effect to douse.

Christ ministered with loving care.
Satan planted seeds of despair.
Christ pursued God's established plan.
Satan then put hate into man.

Christ arrested in the garden.
Satan smiled, said I've got God's Son.
They mocked the Christ and crowned His
    brow.
Satan chortled, I've got Him now.

Death the sentence they did decree.
Satan was ecstatic with glee.
They put Christ's body in a grave.
Satan raved He's now in my cave.

Days marched on, despair for the twelve.
In a gross plan Satan did delve.
The twelve sought guidance what to do.
Satan rejoiced in his great coup.

The third day Christ rose from the dead.
Satan's great joy from him had fled.
As angels shouted out with glee,
Satan proclaimed, oh woe is me.

The Cups

The silver cup of accusation[1]
Then became the cup of salvation.[2]
God had provided His special way
To sustain Israel on that day.

Righteous and wicked, the Lord tests all.
On wicked His snares of rain will fall.
The wicked will have their feast to sup
With fire and brimstone as their full cup.[3]

The Lord is my cup, my all in all.
He supports me, will not let me fall.[4]
My cup of blessings You overfill
And all around Your blessings do spill.[5]

What shall I then to the Lord render
For the benefits He does tender.
The cup of salvation I do raise.
I call on God's name and Him I praise.[6]

Do not look on wine when it is red
For in the cup it sparkles with dread.
It goes down smoothly but then it bites,
Stings like a viper, gives you great frights.[7]

The Lord has taken out of your hand
The cup of reeling His anger planned.
You'll never have to drink it again
But your tormentors that cup will drain.[8]

No consolation cup to provide.
No glad voice of the groom or the bride.[9]
Disobedience's libations –
The cup of wrath for all the nations.[10]

The cup full of wrath God then did hand
To Jeremiah with this command –
Give to the people and make them drink
'Till nary an eye can ever blink.[11]

Babylon's a gold cup in God's hand
Intoxicating all of the land.
The nations drank her wine and were glad
But then the nations were going mad.[12]

The cup of horror, desolation
You will drink and destroy the nation.
You'll drain the cup and gnaw its fragments
And then you will bear your punishments.[13]

A cup will be Jerusalem's plight
Causing reeling to all within sight.
Then Zion will be a heavy stone,
Nations will rage, she'll be overthrown.[14]

Give a cup of cold water to sip
It is part of your discipleship.[15]
You do honor the Christ through this act
And in this world you'll have an impact.

James and John gave to Christ a request.
The Christ presented to them a test.
Then can you drink the cup that I drink
Or from this trial will you then shrink?[16]

Is outside the cup all that you clean
While inside is full of acts so mean?
The inside of the cup you must wash
So the hypocrisy you can squash.[17]

He gave thanks for the cup, gave to all.
My blood of the covenant His call.[18]
Drink heartily, leave nary a drip.
This is part of your discipleship.

They went to the garden there to pray.
While I go farther, here you will stay.
Christ prayed to Abba, let this cup go
Yet only Your will that I must show.[19]

Christ's cup was not the way of the sword,
His Father's will would be His reward.
Return the sword into its scabbard.
For God's will Christ was fully prepared.[20]

Is not the cup of blessing we bless
A sharing of Christ's blood we confess?
We share with the cup and with the bread,
Through this our spirits by Christ are fed.[21]

All who are worshippers of the beast
Will drink God's cup of wine as their feast.
The wine is God's anger and His wrath,
Fire and brimstone their tormented path.[22]

She was adorned in regal array,
Gold cup of uncleanness on display.
Babylon the great, feared by nations,
Mother of all abominations.[23]

Fallen is Babylon the voice said.
Pay back double her deeds on her head.
Great evil from her cup she did pour,
God then doubled His cup to twice more.[24]

With Christ's blood, the blood that they did
    spill,
Salvation's cup the Christ then did fill.
He has redeemed us, called us His own
And His great love for us He has shown.

1. Genesis 44:1-17
2. Genesis 45:1-15
3. Psalm 11:5-6
4. Psalm 16:5
5. Psalm 23:5
6. Psalm 116:12-13
7. Proverbs 23:31-35
8. Isaiah 51:22-23
9. Jeremiah 16:7-9
10. Jeremiah 25:15
11. Jeremiah 25:15-16
12. Jeremiah 51:7
13. Ezekiel 27:31-35
14. Zechariah 12:2-3
15. Matthew 10:42
16. Mark 10:38-39
17. Matthew 23:25-26
18. Mark 14:23-24
19. Mark 14.30
20. John 18:11
21. 1 Corinthians 10:16
22. Revelation 14:10
23. Revelation 17:4-5
24. Revelation 18:6

Tool Box

What do you have in your tool box,
Implements ready for your use?
Are these applied judiciously,
Or are they things that you abuse?

Here are some tools that should be there.
An instruction book's number one.[1]
It should be read and understood
And before any work is done.

A screw driver's a helpful tool,
Its value's often undersung.
Be sure to tighten all loose screws,
Especially those of the tongue.[2]

A hammer is of great value.
Without it the box suffers loss.
Hammer God's precepts in your heart,[3]
Remember Christ nailed to the cross.[4]

The pry-bar is a good lever.
It adds leverage to your pull.
Use it to pry sin from your life[5]
So that with Christ you can be full.

A wrench is a quite handy tool.
It's useful to cinch things up tight
Such as my lips so I don't judge,[6]
And thus with Christ, my words are right.

A saw should be in each tool box.
If your hand causes you to sin[7]
The saw is ready to cut it off.
Though maimed, eternal life you win.

A flashlight is important too.
It puts good light on ev'ry task,
Makes instructions easy to read[8]
Thus less questions you have to ask.

A magnet's a good thing to have
Whatever task you're working on.
It draws us closer to the Christ,[9]
And greater fellowship is won.

A pair of forceps must be there
To pick up pieces that I spy.
And even more importantly
To pluck the log out of my eye.[10]

A tool box is an aide to life.
One thing of which you must be sure.
A tool is there for prevention,
'Cause none of them can bring a cure.

(Written while travelling through Georgia,
on the way to Florida)

---

1. 2 Timothy 3:16
2. James 3:8
3. Matthew 5:13-48
4. John 19:17-18
5. Romans 6:23
6. Matthew 7:1
7. Matthew 5:30
8. Matthew 13:16
9. Hebrews 10:22
10. Matthew 7:5

Shepherd of My Soul

Lord, You're the shepherd of my soul,
It is to You that I belong.
I need Your help, I need Your grace,
It is through You that I am strong.

Take my sinful self in Your arms,
Wash me so that I can be clean.
Inspire my heart, my soul, my mind
That from You about life I'd glean.

Help me to free myself from me
That only on You I'd depend.
Guide all my thoughts and all my ways
So I could truly be Your friend.

(Written while having lunch
at the Hermitage House Smorgasbord)

Appendix One

Answers for the first seven riddles

1. A candle
2. A musical note
3. The sun
4. Hot air balloon
5. Wrist watch
6. Ceiling fan
7. River

Appendix Two

Answer for the eighth riddle

The eighth riddle is found in riddle one.

Each two lines form a couplet . Count the syllables, or beats, for each line. The first pair have 7 syllables, the next pair have 8 syllables, then 9, 10, 11, 10, 9, 8, 7. The numbers increase then reverse and the numbers decrease. This structure is a literary form called a chiasma or chiastic. It is sometimes referred to as stair-step construction. Chiasma is a literary device where a sequence of ideas or elements is presented and then repeated in reverse order, using the same elements or synonyms.

There are many examples of this in the Bible. Psalms is good place to look for them as the Psalms are Hebrew poems. A good example is Psalm 90:1-2 . The psalmist (Moses in this instance) builds his case then reverses the process using synonyms.

Appendix Three

The Brother-Sister Saga
(see p. 34)

If this poem left you wondering, the following may be of assistance. Take a deep breath, then as fast as you can, without stopping, read out loud the last line of the poem.

If the above still leaves you perplexed, the result is presented in the parenthesis below, in reverse order.

(ytipidneres)

www.ingramcontent.com/pod-product-compliance
Lightning Source LLC
Chambersburg PA
CBHW060357050426
42449CB00009B/1775